Burton & Neston History Society

Introduction

In 2011 the CH64 event group raised the idea of a heritage leaflet or booklet which would interest visitors and locals about the history of Neston and surrounding villages.

Community action Neston [CAN] organised a number of meetings with interested groups to develop the idea. The decision was to produce a booklet rather than a leaflet. Members of the Burton and Neston History Society were asked to write different sections of the booklet. These included Anthony Annakin-Smith, Sue Craggs, Clive Edwards, Jerry Harris, Edward Hilditch and Hilary Morris. The project then stalled as external funding to have the booklet printed was withdrawn.

In 2018 the Burton and Neston History Society decided to publish the booklet after Robert Thrift, our publicity secretary, took and added many of the photographs. We hope you will find this booklet an interesting introduction to the history of the area. If you wish to find out more, the history society has published four books. These are, Burton in Wirral, Neston 1840-1940, Neston at War and Neston, Stone Age to Steam Age. The first three books are now out of print but can be borrowed from Neston Library.

    Edward Hilditch
        Chairman Burton and Neston History Society - Nov. 2018

sites.google.com/site/burtonnestonhistory/home   www.nestonpast.com

A Guide to some of Neston's Villages

Great Neston, with its church dedicated to Saint Mary and Saint Helen, was once the main settlement and the centre of Neston parish. In medieval times, and until the nineteenth century, there were seven other small local settlements in the parish, all eight being known as townships. These were Little Neston, Ness, Leighton, Thornton Hough, Raby, Willaston and Ledsham. Four townships became parts of new parishes after 1850. In addition, Parkgate grew up as a port and resort, astride both Great Neston and Leighton. Burton is, with Puddington, in its own parish of St. Nicholas.

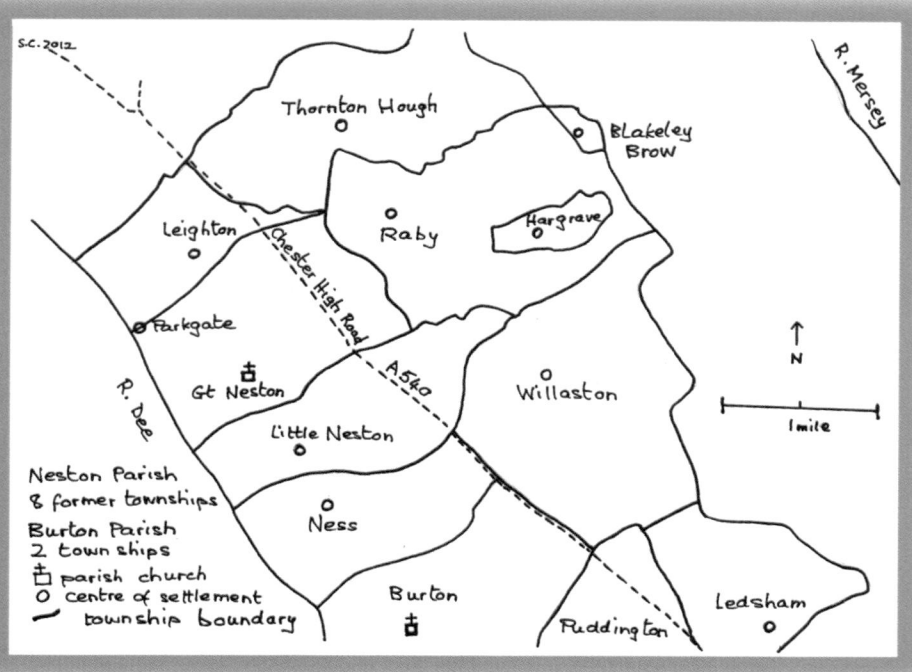

Burton

The name of this village is believed to come from the Saxon, *burgh tun*, or settlement near a fortress. This probably refers to its Iron Age hill fort, situated on the shore of the River Dee about a mile from the village centre. The fort and the land around it were bought by the RSPB in 2009. No stonework survives, only earthworks, similar to small forts in North Wales. The RSPB now owns reed beds, wet grassland and fens which support an amazing array of wild life. These can be seen from the visitor's centre or along the network of trails. Further details can be found at *rspb.org.ok/burtonmerewetlands*.

In medieval times, Burton was in the estates of the diocese of Lichfield, then the cathedral for this part of Northern England. A hospital of St. Andrew was established for travellers and sick people at Denhall by Lichfield diocese, and run by their own hospital of St. John. After the Reformation, the hospital buildings became a small farm, and later disappeared. Its site is known, and one of its boundary stones is preserved in the grounds of Burton Manor, with the inscription St J H.

In 1650, nearby Denhall House was the scene of a tragedy. Edward Dunsterville of Raby, a minister of the Church of Ireland, returned to Wirral with his wife, Lucy, having been exposed to bubonic plague in Dublin. As recorded at the time, *'Upon there landinge in Englande [they] came to a house called Denwall House in Wirral, where they remained shut up for a tyme, in witch tyme the said Edward Dunsterville dyed and the said Luce Dunsterville, the next day or night dyed after him.'*

The parish church is dedicated to St. Nicholas, the patron saint of sailors. Like those of so many local villages, its men were often associated with the sea, and owned or crewed small trading vessels of less than 100 tons, which traded along the coast and further afield. Although most of the church, including the one-handed clock, dates from around 1721, there are still a few fragments of earlier

stonework. The large group of early table tombs carry devices such as skull and crossbones, or hour glasses, which were part of the seventeenth century's symbolism for mortality. In the woods behind the churchyard are graves said to be of Quakers, now eroded, and dated 1663. The stones, however, are not typical of Quaker memorials.

Burton Manor is the 1904 remodelling in sandstone of an earlier brick mansion, built around 1805. Its site was the early nineteenth century home of the Congreve family, who succeeded Lichfield Diocese as landlords of the village in 1805. They sold Burton Hall in 1902 to Henry Neville Gladstone, the third son of the famous William Gladstone, Liberal Prime Minister. Henry Neville constructed the present Manor, before selling it in 1924. After a number of different uses the manor became an adult education college in 1948 for Wirral, Cheshire and Liverpool until its closure by the owner, Liverpool Council in 2011. The house and several of its outbuildings are Grade II listed.

'Auricula theatre' in the walled garden

Following closure of the college, the Manor has been largely unoccupied, while its ownership and future purpose has been the subject of protracted negotiation. Sadly, this delay has been to the significant detriment of the condition of the building. Completion of sale to a new owner took place in February 2018. Its new owners, The Burton Manor Restoration Company, put forward plans in May 2018 (gaining approval in September 2018) to convert the Manor to office space and build 17 houses on the part of the site that formed the college. The houses will be sold on a freehold basis to finance the restoration and future upkeep of the manor and so secure its future.

Throughout this time a group of volunteers have continued to manage the garden and restored the Victorian walled kitchen garden and green houses. The Atelier, a group of craft work-shops, occupies some of the out buildings.

A nineteenth century underground ice house has recently been restored and can be visited. Bishop Wilson's birthplace in 1663 is the thatched sandstone cottage opposite the Manor. He became Bishop of Sodor and Man, giving his name to the local primary school.

The restored, grade II listed sandstone ice house

Great Neston

Great Neston has some evidence of Viking settlement or influence, in the form of five carved stones. These had been buried under an aisle of the church, found during its restoration, and are now displayed for visitors in the church. Place and field names may also include Scandinavian origins. Neston in Doomsday in 1086 possessed a priest,

suggesting a church was already here. It was reconstructed in the Middle Ages. The church was again rebuilt in 1875 after it was found that the structure was unsafe. Only the medieval tower and the stone fragments remain from the earlier building. Houses and inns in the High Street date from the eighteenth centuries, and the barn of the Brewers' Arms may be the oldest surviving structure after the church. There is an 18th century sundial above Gittins's Carpet Shop in the High Street. Elsewhere there are several other date stones with the initials of the couples for whom the houses were built. The most prominent is above the newsagents on the cross with the date 1724. The initials are of Thomas and Margery Whittell. Thomas was a important Neston brewer and he died in 1758. Vine House opposite the library on Parkgate Road also displays a sundial on its front wall *(right)*.

Neston developed as an important seafaring out-port of Chester, its heyday being about 1550 to 1700. After this, it declined because of changes in the depth of the River Dee, the increasing draft of the larger sailing ships, and then the effects of the canal cut into the tidal Dee. Ships moored in the deep-water anchorages, especially at Beer House Hole in Parkgate, near to the current Boat House Inn. Smaller craft could beach on the sloping sands where Parkgate Parade is now situated.

During this time of prosperity, Neston and Parkgate were connected by trade to North Wales, Ireland, Europe and the Mediterranean. Olive oil jars were found in the excavations in Neston on the site of Sainsbury's supermarket. The New Key was built in the sixteenth century and associated walls are still visible in the fields at the end of Old Quay Lane.

Remains of the 'New Key' near Old Quay Lane

Nestor's port eventually fell into disuse as Liverpool developed into the main deep-water port for the North West.

Famous men and women associated with the parish include Lady Hamilton, born in Ness, and George Frederick Handel, who returned to England via Parkgate after giving the first performance of his new oratorio Messiah in Dublin. John Wesley, founder of Methodism, visited Neston several times in April 1762, and commented, '*I preached at the small house they have just built and the hearers were remarkable serious.*' J.M.W. Turner painted the landscape over the Dee when he visited Parkgate. Christopher Bushell, a merchant from Liverpool, built Hinderton Hall on the main Chester Road, and took an active part in

Hinderton Hall, Chester Road

reforming the old Victorian life of Neston, by improving the water and sewerage services. The traffic island with the old drinking fountain replaces the water pump he installed. The original supply was contaminated, and so was later replaced when the new water mains were installed.

Railways first came to Neston in 1866 with the construction of the branch line from Hooton to Parkgate. This line was extended to West Kirby in 1886 and is now the Wirral Way A replacement footbridge in Neston was installed in 2001, to carry the path over Bridge Street. The Bidston to Wrexham line, which runs through Neston was opened in 1896. This line still operates. The former station master's house, now a private dwelling, is on Liverpool Road.

Neston's market charter of 1728 was granted when Sir Roger Mostyn was the land owner of Leighton and Great Neston. It traded in the area now occupied by the Victorian drinking fountain and the top part of Parkgate Road. This area is called The Cross, not because of a market cross, but because it was the main cross road in Neston. After a lapse, the market was re-established in the 20th century by the local authority. Since Sainsbury's was built in 2010, the market has continued to be held weekly on Fridays, in a newly paved market square near to the previous site.

At times, a Farmers' Market has been held in the square. Instead of the old annual fair there is now a fun fair, in the week of the Ladies' Walk, which takes place on the first Thursday afternoon in June.

Fun fair on Ladies' day in June 2015

Since 1314, the Neston Female Friendly Society has walked through the street in procession. Participants, including many children, carry flowers mounted on staves. At the front of the procession is a large banner carried by men and followed by a band. The people in the procession go to a service in the parish church.

Edward Pryce Lloyd Mostyn sold his Wirral estates in 1849, to fund a project at Llandudno. His ancestral property, Leighton Hall, already tenanted by farmers, and Great Neston passed into several hands at a series of large auction sales.

Among the buildings in the centre of Neston was the site of the vicarage, which was shown on the 1732 Mostyn estate map. After 1857 it became a girl's school. After the building was demolished the local grocery chain, Irwin's, built a shop which in 1960 became Tesco's. The first state school was opened in the style of the Church National Schools, near to the Malt Shovel public house. It was converted into apartments in around 2000.

Ledsham

This outpost of Neston parish lay on the southern edge of the eight original villages. It became part of the new parish of Capenhurst in the 1850s.

While of great interest to historians, and an attractive former farming village, it has little to offer visitors apart from a plant nursery. A former Ledsham inhabitant is buried in Neston churchyard near to the modern south west porch, his simple stone labelled *"John Hancock of Ledsham Dec 1st 1775 Aged 112"*. He may be one of the inhabitants who took part in a "beating of the bounds" to learn the boundaries of the township, recorded in the early eighteenth century.

Court Farm, Ledsham

The southern edge of Ledsham is still obvious, as a narrow belt of tall trees. Residents, while officially required to attend Neston parish church for important services, were allowed to go to Shotwick, which was nearer to their homes.

After the First World War, the village was bought by Cheshire County Council, as part of its project to rent out small holdings to families needing a livelihood. Most of the houses and barns are now converted to modern cottages. Two barns showed their late medieval origins by their cruck beam construction. As all the properties are private, little can be seen by a visitor.

A quarry said to have supplied the stone for Capenhurst's Victorian church became a pond, then an allotment garden. This can be seen over the gate next to Rose Cottage, a delightful eighteenth century house next to the Church. The house was built on the solid rock, and probably incorporates earlier material.

Holy Trinity Church, Capenhurst

Willaston

For most of its existence the village was a closely knit and largely self-contained community, obtaining its livelihood almost entirely from agriculture. Old farmhouses and other buildings from its past survive, restored and altered for new uses as private houses or commercial premises.

Near the Green, the Old Hall has stone mullioned and transomed windows and a stone entrance porch. Opposite stands the half-timbered Old Red Lion, a public house until 1928, forming an attractive background to any organised activities that take place on the Green. The Nag's Head, not many yards away, was built in 1733.

Willaston Old Hall, Hadlow Road

And the Pollard Inn *(left)*, at the south-west corner of the Green until later buildings encroached upon the open space, was originally a farmhouse called Corner House Farm, with an ancient stone wing.

On the south side of the Green, the Memorial Hall, originally "Willaston Literary Institute, Reading Room and Library", built in 1892, has been thoroughly renovated and is an asset to the village.

Willaston Memorial Hall

Willaston's Anglican church was built in 1855, but until 1865 the village was one of the eight townships of the ancient parish of Neston. The present Methodist chapel, in Neston Road, dating from 1889, replaced one built in 1838 on land behind Cherry Brow Terrace. The first Willaston school, originally consisting of only one room, was built in 1859 on the Green. The present school was opened in 1930. The old school was then demolished, and on 6 May 1935, on part of its former site, the copper beech tree was planted to commemorate the Silver Jubilee of King George V and Queen Mary.

A branch railway line from Hooton to Parkgate and West Kirby was opened in 1866, but it was eventually found to be uneconomic, and it was closed to passengers in 1956, and to freight in 1962. The track was later taken up, and the linear Wirral Country Park was opened in 1973. Hadlow Road Station has been refurbished as one of the places of interest in the park and re-creates the appearance of an old station.

Outside the village proper stands the mill, the largest of the Wirral windmills, which dates from 1800 and once provided substantial employment for the village. In 1930, when the sails were damaged and sawn off, work at the mill stopped. One of its millstones now forms the main feature of the village sign on the Little Green

Willaston Mill (looking east on Mill Lane)

Little Neston

About one mile from Great Neston lies the former farming settlement of Little Neston. It still has an attractive centre, with several old farm houses. Number 26 The Green was an inn called the Durham Ox, bearing the date 1731, and the initials H and AB, probably commemorating a rebuild by Hugh and Anne Bennett.

right: former Durham Ox

The Royal Oak was a thatched building which burnt down in 1901 and was replaced by the current building. White House Farm is dated 1732 with the initials of George and Jane Bedson. Other old houses near to the centre are The Rocklands of 1700, and Mellock Farm.

The Methodist Church in the centre was built in 1872 at a cost of £645.13s.3d and the church hall was extended three times in the 1960's and 1970's. The Roman Catholic church of St. Winefride on Burton Road *(below)* was opened in 1843 in a school built two years before, designed

by Augustus Pugin. A window commemorates Father Plessington of Puddington Hall who was executed in 1679 at Chester and was the priest to the catholic family resident at Puddington Old Hall in the seventeenth century.

Neston's Cottage Hospital operated between 1920 and 1964, one of its beds being dedicated by his friends to Second Lieutenant Gunn VC, who died in World War 2. The commemorative plaque was removed to Neston parish church when the hospital was closed and demolished.

There is a busy street of small shops and businesses in Town Lane, which leads to the village green. In spring, the central grass areas are covered with multi-coloured crocus flowers.

Like Great Neston and Ness, Little Neston had many inhabitants who worked in the local coal mines during the two centuries up to 1928.

Ness

Ness is another village of farms, and once had two tithe barns. These held tax payments in kind, mainly farm produce, given to the church. One farm is still working, Goldstraw Farm, with large glacial boulders at the gate to protect the walls from cart wheels. Other farms have been converted into homes. The Old Bakery and the village shop closed in the twentieth century.

The public house, The Wheatsheaf *(left)*, stands on the site of a Victorian brick building. There was a well-known plough works, making horse-drawn ploughs, owned by the Mealor family. They held patents to the ploughs they developed, which were sold all over Britain. The workshop operated as a lawn mower service shop until its conversion to cottages in 2009, now called

Mealor's Court. One of the Mealor family, a devout Methodist, turned up at church on the day the hour went forward. Missing the service, he demanded that it should be repeated for his benefit!

The most famous inhabitant of Ness, but briefly, was Amy or Emma Lyon, whose baptism was registered in Neston Parish church. Her father, a blacksmith, died and her family moved to Hawarden when she was a few months old. In London, she worked as a nurse maid and later became well known as the mistress of Lord Nelson, and the wife of Lord Hamilton.

On the road from Ness to Burton lies Ness Botanic Gardens, started in 1898 by Arthur K. Bulley, a Liverpool cotton merchant. At his family home, Mickwell Brow, the gardens reflected his collections of exotic shrubs and flowers, and became a showcase for his nationwide business, Bees Seeds, located later in Sealand. In 1948, his daughter, Lois Bulley, gave the estate to the University of Liverpool.

The herbaceous lawn, Ness Gardens

It is now run as a public garden, now regarded as one of the best for tourists to visit in this area. The water garden contains some of the alpine plants brought back by plant collectors, such as George Forrest, sponsored by Bulley. Forrest brought back the first specimen of *Pieris forrestii*, which grows in the northern shrubbery at Ness.

Thornton Hough

Seven Stars public house

The name of Thornton comes from the early English for a thorn tree farm. Hough is the family name of a lord of the manors of Leighton and Thornton in the 1530s.

There were two early manor houses, both now vanished. The village itself in 1847 was described as *"presenting a very unpleasant appearance, and though it possesses a few tolerably good houses, the greater portion are of a very inferior description"*. Two years later, the local land owners, the Mostyns of Mostyn in Flintshire, sold all their Cheshire estates. The Earl of Shrewsbury owned part of the rest. Joseph Hirst, a Yorkshire

textile manufacturer, chose to live in Thornton Hough in the 1860s. He built All Saints Anglican church in 1867 *(above)* and had a fifth clock face added to its tower, because he could not see the lower face from his house. He also built the vicarage, a school, and Wilshaw Terrace, a row of cottages and shops.

He died in 1874 and the estate was bought by William Hesketh Lever, who in 1917 became the first Lord Leverhulme, the owner of the Sunlight Soap works in Port Sunlight. He rebuilt almost the whole of the rest of the village, using architects employed by him at Port Sunlight. He replaced the existing house at Thornton Manor for his residence and built St. George's Congregational church in 1906 in a superb

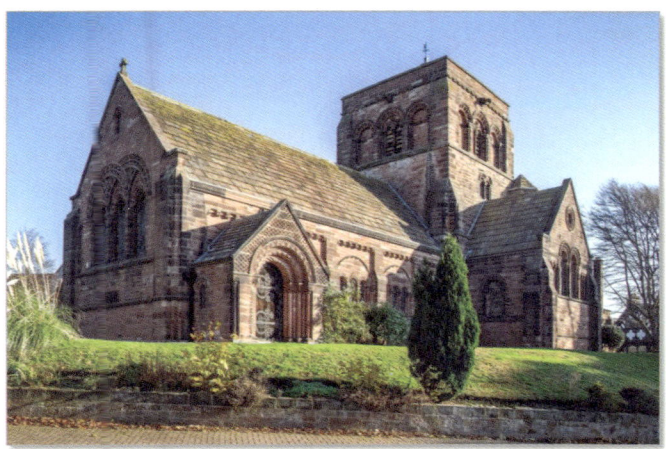

Romanesque style, now the United Reformed Church *(left)*.

Villagers recall family memories of the sports days organised by the first Lord Leverhulme, with races, cycle competitions and greasy pole climbs, in the spirit of old village fairs.

For the millennium, a gateway was built to the village green and sports ground, in half-timbered traditional style.

Today it's a joy to walk round this model village, with its village green, and the old blacksmith's forge. Visitors can look for the two churches and admire the huge entrance arch to Thornton Manor on the road towards Brimstage. Footpaths skirting the grounds of the manor give a small impression of the woodlands there. Thornton Hough has a cheerful public house, The Seven Stars, older than most of the present cottages. The Thornton Hall hotel, and the Red Fox restaurant, previously called the Grange, all provide fine dining.

Houses on Raby Road, Thornton Hough

Raby

Raby has for centuries stayed largely unchanged in its layout and general appearance, except for the motorway and the newer houses around Raby Mere, adjoining Bromborough on the east.

The name Raby means village on the boundary and it is believed to be one of the Wirral Viking settlements, denoted by its 'by' ending. Near its centre lies Hargrave, an enclave of Little Neston, centred around Hargrave Hall Farm. There are also two more small isolated portions of Little Neston on Raby's eastern boundary. The Raby estates were held by the monks of St. Werbugh's abbey in Chester, eventually by the Earls of Shrewsbury, remaining with the Earl until sold 1911.

Raby was a part of the Forest of Wirral. This was not a forest, but a hunting area for the privileged Norman rulers. Large areas were probably like Thurstaston Common is today, a mixture of heath land and woods. The forest laws were very restrictive to the local farmers, in order to protect the hunting of deer.

Raby Mere was probably created to power the water mill which worked here from at least the seventeenth century. The Mill House, still occupied, has a date stone of 1601, and the sluice for the reservoir lies under the road at one end of the lake. In the late 19th and early 20th

centuries Raby Mere was a very popular place to visit, with rowing boats, refreshment rooms and amusements. Now the mere is a tranquil place, and the water mill's wheel and walls are lost under the bank to the left of the Mill House.

From medieval times the people of Raby and Hargrave attended Neston church. Each household had its allotted pews, and Raby shared the costs of providing a church warden. This came to an end in 1868, when the new Church of All Saints was opened in Thornton Hough. The social focus of Raby then increasingly looked to Thornton Hough.

Until about 1750, there was a little church school on the south side of

the former Victorian Raby school house

Quarry Road, Neston, which also served Raby children. In 1877 Joseph Hirst of Thornton Manor built a school house in Raby for the children, this later becoming the Men's Club. It was sold by the church to become a private dwelling in the 1990s.

Coal Mining in Neston

Near the Harp public house was once the largest industrial site in the district, partly in Ness and partly in Little Neston. The first atmospheric steam engine in Wirral and West Cheshire pumped water from the coal mine tunnels. Opened in 1759, the earliest mine was at its peak in the 1770s and 1780s.

A second mine was opened in 1819. There was bitter rivalry between two of the mines' owners, Sir Thomas Stanley and Thomas Cottingham, the latter living in Glenton House in Little Neston village. The quarrels became violent, resulting in acts of sabotage including deliberate damage to one of the mine tunnels under the River Dee. A witness claimed that Stanley's agent gave orders to his workers that 'If they met with any of Cottingham's men, they must break their heads' or lose their jobs. After two court cases, Thomas Cottingham won the dispute, with £2000 compensation from the Stanley family. Some of the mine's tunnels were designed as underground canals, flooded so as to take narrow boats. These boat tunnels extended about a mile under the

river Dee, one at a depth of almost 300 feet. The boats, laden with coal from the face, were moved through the tunnels by men "walking" them with their feet along the tunnel ceiling.

The early mines were closed by 1855. However, a new shaft was sunk in 1875 on the other side of Marshlands Road, where the colliery office is now converted into a private house. The mine's pumps removed salt water which filtered from the estuary through the rocks into the workings. Twelve years later, the company was producing 100 000 tons of coal annually. Three hundred people were employed by the early 1920s. Closure, however, came in 1927.

Working conditions were extremely hard for adults and children employed in the mines. In 1841, there were seven boys aged 9 to 14 working underground. A miner recalled, 'At the end of the First World War my father retired ... suffering from miners' blindness, which was caused by being underground so long ... He cut the coal and his brother filled the boxes, which held 10 cwt of coal. They came home with 21 shillings a week for the two of them. They worked a six-day week, 48 hours a week.'

Over the years the mines were open dozens of men and boys were killed. The colliery accident book between 1911 and 1927 records the deaths of William Briscoe, William Barnes, Thomas Hughes, Richard Roberts, William Jones and Frederick Abel. Relatives of the miners live in the Neston area to this day and attended a 250th anniversary open air memorial service for those who lost their lives.

Denhall Quay, its stones still standing, was used to export Neston coal to Ireland in the eighteenth and early nineteenth century. William Lawson built his cottage on the quay nearly hundred years ago, and was succeeded there by Fred Jones, a wild-fowler.

Two descriptive boards mounted at the end of Marshlands Road and at Denhall Quay give details of the phases of local coal mining. A branch railway line was once linked with the Hooton to West Kirby railway to carry away coal and survives in part as a footpath west of Neston. While little remains to be seen of the mines, the public footpath along the Dee shore provides a pleasant walk, and a view of the estuary's birds. A National Cycle Network route connects this path to the Welsh boundary south of Burton and Shotwick.

Parkgate

Parkgate's river front is a delightful mixture of buildings, resembling many old seaports, even though its position overlooks not the open ocean, but the tidal river, with Wales in the background. Houses, cafes, pubs and shops, along with the one-time Assembly Rooms in Balcony House, crowd together along the The Parade facing the sea wall promenade. Small lanes or weints run back among the buildings from the main road, which follows the river shore. At one time, small boats and lighters could beach on the tidal sand in front of the houses, to carry cargoes from ships anchored further away in the main channel of the river Dee. The original path of the River Dee ran closer the shore than today, with a deeper pool at the north end, known as Beerhouse Hole in early sailing charts. The Boat House public house is a relatively new building on the site of the old Beerhouse.

St. Thomas's Church, Mostyn Square

Occupying part of the medieval deer park of Neston, which was enclosed in about 1250, and near to one of its gates, Parkgate did not exist until the seventeenth century. The port grew up in parts of the two older townships, Leighton and Great Neston, along the shore line. The boundary between the two townships lies in Mostyn Square where St Thomas' church now stands.

The Beerhouse, at the north end of Parkgate's front, is marked on Greenvile Collins' chart of the Dee, surveyed in 1686 so is probably one of the earliest buildings. A pier of the site of the present Boathouse was the point of departure for ferries to Bagillt, Flint and Point of Ayr. Until about 1815, when the last Irish packet ships sailed, Parkgate was an important port for both cargoes and passengers. A customs house stood at the south end of The Parade, its site near the present Old Quay public house. The Customs office was demolished when the new public house was built in 1963.

A Watch House, still standing further north, was another part of the excise and coastguard facilities of the late eighteenth century port. Smuggling was rife, but probably lacking in drama, with small amounts of tea, alcoholic drinks, and spices brought in by ships engaged also in regular trade, hidden in local cellars. There are many entirely untrue tales of underground tunnels, connecting impossibly distant places with the shore. The Customs and Excise were still kept busy, however.

"The Watch House" Parkgate c1913   YW1-1

In the eighteenth century, Parkgate's status as a port for Ireland was nationally important. Its success was sometimes threatened by the varying weather and difficult winds in the mouth of the River Dee. The land route to the rival port for Ireland at Holyhead was too difficult and mountainous, unless the delay of waiting for a suitable wind in the Dee proved unbearably frustrating. An eighteenth-century wall painting of a ship in the tropics is preserved in one of houses on the front, probably a reflection of Parkgate vessels' occasional journeys to southern Europe and the southern states of America.

As well as the shipping trade, the fashion for sea bathing for its health benefits led to many visitors coming to Parkgate from the mid 1700's. Lady Hamilton visited in 1784 to treat a skin complaint.

The first part of the sea wall from the Watch House to the Assembly Rooms was constructed by 1814 (no Donkey Stand yet), followed by the southern section from the Assembly Rooms to South Slip, just beyond the Customs House. Next the northern part from the Watch

House to Pengwern Arms (now the Boathouse Inn) and finally the length near the wide section at the Donkey Stand was completed by around 1840. Inland the long straight Rope Walk had been constructed enabling ropes to be made to support local shipping.

Parkgate enjoyed a time of success as a fishing village, aided by the new rail links, but fishing boats were forced to move down river to catch flatfish and the famous Parkgate shrimps. These were once caught near Parkgate, later off Thurstaston, as the salt marshes grew, and since then off the North Wales coast.   *below: view across the marsh at sunset*

Mostyn House School contributed a very recognisable black and white frontage to the landscape.

Moved here from Tarvin in 1855, this respected public school was run for several generations by the Grenfell family, and closed in 2009.

There were several small boarding schools here in the last two centuries, advertising healthy air as well as education.

Parkgate remains a popular visiting place on summer evenings and weekends. Nicholls's shop has made ice cream since the 1930s and eating an ice cream cone while admiring the view over the marshes to Wales at sunset time is a memorable experience.

Burton & Neston History Society   First published 2013, revised 2016 and 2018